DIAMOND SONNETS

The Pangs of a Bachelor Soul

AROKIYA DASS

INDIA · SINGAPORE · MALAYSIA

ISBN 979-8-89415-312-4

To my parents and siblings, for the source of inspiration...

Table of Contents

Summary of the Book

Diamond, though costlier than gold, preferred less due to its availability and usage. But these diamond sonnets are more valuable not only to me but also to all those who read them with a passion to find value in one life. Hence, it is like a diamond piece that radiates when it is worn, these sonnets will kindle the minds and hearts of the readers. Diamonds represent eternal love, which is why they are usually offered as engagement and wedding rings. Like the diamond, the sonnets symbolize understanding and love that are expressed in each of the topics. They also signify the characteristics of a diamond along with the reader's inner nature.

It is my belief and practice that to vibe with other cultures, creeds, customs, and concerns, one has to be part and parcel of the system where one can celebrate with, live with, and feel with others. I thank the divine for showering me with gifts of picking up other languages that are not my mother tongue. Indeed, it was due to the exposure to different parts of India as part of my training both in the secular and religious arena due to the way of life I chose to live. At one of the stages of formation, in order to exhibit the outcome of our learning, we were asked to pen down poems, prose, stories, and jokes for the periodicals published by the scholastics in the training. As it was a mandatory process, I used to write poems based on certain topics following a style similar to Shakespeare's sonnets. Invariably, it helped me to build my English vocabulary, to understand and to communicate English in an efficient way which boosted my confidence. I did not continue the spirit of writing since it was not mandatory but focused on acquiring expertise in other chosen subjects.

As the years rolled by, a crazy thought haunted me to pen down certain life experiences in the form of the sonnets. Hence, I started jotting down a couple of sonnets which enthused me to write more on some more interesting topics. When I shared these sonnets with one of the professors who teaches English Literature at XIM University, appreciated my writings, suggested the genre of the sonnets besides my own knowledge of it, and encouraged me to publish the sonnets in a book form. Hence, I started writing the sonnets strictly adhering to the nomenclatures on different topics.

There are ten chapters down the line, they are not scripted in any type of sequence but based on alphabetical order of the titles. Each chapter except for two chapters consists of five sonnets and throws light into the particular aspect of life experience. Chapter One focuses on Impeccable Initiatives comprising my village, my first school, the church I attended, the teachers who taught me, and a six-kilometer stretch road to the high school in which I walked and pedaled for four years. Chapter Two is themed on Jubilant Junctures – referring to major and significant celebrations in life like birthdays, religious initiations, marriage, anniversaries, and partying farewells.

Chapter Three is based on the topic of Masked Masterminds stressing the important roles played by the organs in our body without being perceived by our stripped eyes. Chapter Four is jotted down on the topic – Mesmerizing Memories describing how I deviated from the decisions of my parents, the grief-filled first flight journey, the seven months stay in Goa as part of a training program, the behavioral activities of the ignorant moments innocently committed, and a month-long hospital experiment in Kolkata with the Missionaries of Charity. Indeed, recollecting and cherishing the experiences as a memory while I was writing down enhanced my lifestyle.

In Chapter Five, I emphasized the importance of nature which nurtures as well as hinders us at times through different seasons. Though the seasons exhibit diverse roles in varied geographical locations, the cyclical process must take place for sustainable development. Chapter Six depicts a number of Passionate Professions among hundreds of careers undertaken for the individual as well as community progress and service. At times, certain professions may sound unfavorable to some people. But every profession plays certain roles in the general society for smooth functioning.

The subject of psychology entices marketing companies to capitalize on the worth of building the brands of products and services. As the mind is patterned in a fixed way based on the behavior of the beholders, it also needs to be tamed to accept and adjust to the situations, people, and events. Chapter Seven depicts the Psychosomatic Sensations of a person and his/her actions and reactions accordingly. We are interrelated and interdependent social beings. In fact, relationships are the basic aspects of our sustenance. Chapter Eight illustrates about ten types of persons an individual experienced in his family under the title – 'Rejuvenating Relationships'. Besides dramatizing the characteristics of the persons, their impact on the person in a subtle way is shown to the readers.

The sonnets in Chapter Nine are dedicated to the 'Uniqueness of the Universe' which narrate the five elements of the universe under attractive headings as follows: Enigmatically Embroidered = The Earth, Lucrative Life-giver = The Water, Blazing Brightness = The Fire, Flowing Force = The Air and Enchanting Ecstasy = The Ether. Of course, it was a simple attempt to put into 14 lines each about the greatness and grandeur of the universal elements. In the final Chapter Ten, the sonnets are unique to a person who lives a life with a special vocation under a religious order based on vows. That is why the topic of the chapter – Valued Virtues and Vitiating Vices consists of the following five sonnets namely Choicest Charity = Vow of Chastity, Passionate Pledge = Vow of Poverty, Observed Obeisance = Vow of Obedience, Gracious Grants = 7 Gifts of the Holy Spirit, and Dreaded Desires = 7 Deadly Sins itself is very peculiar to the readers to visualize and to understand the lifestyle of religious people and their ethos.

Acknowledgement

Indeed, he is closer to me than I am to myself. Hence, first and foremost, I thank HIM – the Almighty for the gift of life and steadfast love received from him in and through his images in numerous ways and forms. I am grateful to the Lord for His immeasurable blessing upon my life. I do not find enough words to express my gratitude to my parents for their unconditional care and concern. Yet I express my indebtedness to my parents though Dad has taken heavenly birth long back, to my beloved Mom, siblings, nieces and nephews, kith, and kin for the source of inspiration.

I remain ever grateful to my teachers, professors, friends, comrades, and well-wishers for their benevolent and insightful thoughts and words, instilling a love for learning, and igniting the imagination to aim high in the course of interactions and interpretations of life experiences and during learning and training periods.

It is my obligation to thank the provincials, superiors, and formators of the Society of Jesus (Jesuits) for lavishly nurturing me intellectually, spiritually, physically, socially, and eco-friendly with their love and affection, inculcating in me the values of discipline, dedication, and determination, and exposing me to varied training and development in order to equip myself for the mission.

As a true leader, always guided me and facilitated the process with the solutions whenever needed for the problems that I faced, either personal or institutional. I thank the Vice Chancellor, Dr. Fr. Anthony R Uvari, SJ, XIM University for his absolute assistance in all my endeavors to excel better and higher with the Jesuits Magis "Semper Excelsius" – ever higher. I express my gratitude to Fr. S. Anthony Joseph Raj, SJ, the Registrar of XIM University for his unwavering support.

As it was stated: brains, like hearts, go where they are appreciated. I express my gratitude to Prof. Lourdes Vijayan, Department of English, XIM University for his magnanimous help and suggestions to pen down my life experiences into sonnets, supplementing flesh to the bonny sonnets and meticulously giving a poetry genre to the sonnets. In fact, it was him who after going through a couple of the sonnets, motivated me to write more sonnets and publish them into a book. Thanks to him for doing the editorial work of the sonnet poems.

I am grateful to Mr. Tapan Kumar Dash, Mr. Kausik Swain and Mr. Subhrajyoti Praharaj for extending with enchanting and appropriate pictures to give extra glamour to the sonnets. As Barry Long stated, acknowledgment is the only way to keep love alive. I am indebted to staff members on both campuses of XIM University for their cooperation and collaboration in all my endeavors. Thank you, readers, for showing interest in this book – a collection of sonnets depicting the varied experiences of a vowed and a bachelor soul!

CHAPTER 1

IMPECCABLE INITIATIVES

1.1 Valiantly Vibrant Village – My Origin

1.2 Highfliers Heritage – My School

1.3 Constant Chanting – My Church Bell

1.4 Mesmerizing Masters – My School Teachers

1.5 Elegantly Enticing – My High School Road

1.1

Valiantly Vibrant Village – My Origin

Wow! What a hamlet, surrounded by greeneries of diversity in all directions!
The east, with paddy, sugarcane, and a rainwater lake for slaking the cattle.
Manmade ponds of west for multiuse with Kharif and Rabi crops rations.
A shrubby brook in north, and in south, cash crops like cultivation battle.

Religious faith structures and sanctuaries dedicated to gods and saints,
Spotted strategically but interspaced as though mutually resolved amid.
Like the thread, the saree too, ascribes to the lush hamlet full of paints,
With exhibitionist nature, flaking with echoing music rowdily avid.

Kindled by intelligence and expertise, educated the ardent ignorant.
Demanded amenities and conveniences – with unwavering one voice.
Networked out of the hamlet in the hope of inspiring future advancement,
Innovation erupted at homes in the enlightened like wildfire with choice.

Oh, hamlet then, altering into an enormous village with provisions,
Despite nobility, the buds lacked excellence due to impulsive revolutions.

1.2

Highfliers Heritage – My School

Bygone, but the memories linger as fresh as a wolfish net from a beck,
Housing the students safely and a spacious staff room, typically gold old.
Roofed with interlocking tiles; slippery, cemented floor with a squared neck,
Cloistered with walls with patriots' portraits, and maps from village to world.

Greenly trees, horned shrubs, and wild creepers characterize the wild around.
Spacious to run hither thither and sessions, delighting in nature's benevolence.
Strolled on the boundary, exhibiting valor and agility by balancing tricks abound,
Spent leisurely and brainstorming on the grounds with confreres' acceptance.

Mulling the teachers even today for creating scare coupled with excitement,
For knowledge by percolating facts and figures filled with ardent notions.
Rarely peers fondling though fought on issues with follies' incitement,
But sorted out before reaching the ears of the class teacher for any oration.

Indelible ejaculation the tables and poems riotously with rhyme and rhythm,
Implanting in the minds hope to prosper and excel even the school anthem.

1.3

Constant Chanting – My Church Bell

A mixture of brace and copper hanging erect elegantly at a tall spire.
Symbolizing the actions by beckoning auspicious time and occasion.
Correlating the belling with specific events either to perspire or to inspire.
Feeling residents, for both sacred and secular, bliss, and gloomy celebration.

Rang periodically to remember the Almighty for the advantageous acts.
Heard as a child the ring thrice a day – signifying time and occasions.
Banged only an abnormal way alerting the untoward events of facts.
Summoned those in the fields and forests to haste with belonging.

Emotions erupt; thoughts trigger, memories elicit and blood stream throb.
Interlinks the divine and the human without lyrics, but moving fervently
Frighten with imposing gloom at a gapped stroke, at the sacred chants snub.
Portentous each blow as daunting either an affluence or misery inadvertently.

Elegantly elucidating mysteries with divine and corporal to the mortal
Silently traversing the faith secrecies hidden underneath although brutal.

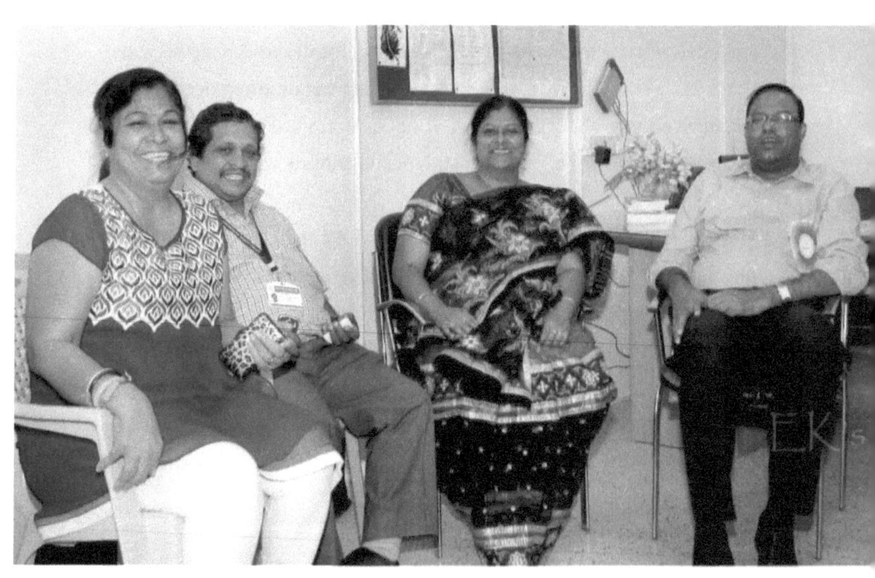

1.4

Mesmerizing Masters – My School Teachers

O Passionate Teachers – molders from first to eighth standard entrants.
Remember not the lessons but a few poems, basic math, and beating.
But retain in vividly the characters that infused into the minds of aspirants.
The willpower, dedication, and discipline leading to successful living.

Ignite budding minds with simple gestures and attitudes with ineligible marks!
More than the lessons grasped, cherishing the ambiance with responsibility.
Electrified with anecdotes and incidents only to inspire and avoid folly larks.
Passionately tickling the futures imbibe morality thereby shaping personality.

Though traveled by bicycle to conduct the classes as a noble profession.
Upholding punctuality and regularity in the daily routine of boredom.
Fatigued, resumed the teaching either by standing or strolling or scription.
Enthused pupils with spontaneous jokes at naughty nuts with filial freedom.

O Teachers, a philosopher, a guide, a friend, and above all a surrogate parent
The bond of an amalgamated relationship remains forever transparent!

1.5

Elegantly Enticing – My High School Road

As the memory toddles along the archaic, twisted, and bumpy road;
The green cultivations, hoary and pale trees, oxygenizing the voyagers.
Decades rolled, paths smoothed, the seven miles carry ranging heavy load,
From the hamlet to the urban, the whole day as fabulous and fervent carriers
Rambled, sprinted, and galloped for miles at the peak of the gallivanting youth.
Reached the school not heeding the assault of social and entrancing nature
No vehicles with two or four-wheel piloted on the messy and grassy path
Bicycled on the solitary way causing no pollution but nurturing side by pasture.

Superstitious spots along the way probing opinions and faith for its foundation
The mind meandered beyond the horizon to grasp the aphorisms of the phase.
No solutions but bedeviled with illusory propositions of the mystic location.
Ages sprang by, evoked by the subconscious subtlety without any base.

Oh, road, jagged housed by belief centers on both sides on phased distance,
Matured, yet empathetic to passersby not doused into any pit even in trance.

CHAPTER 2

JUBILANT JUNCTURES

2.1

Blissful Birthday

Day of gratitude to Trinity – besides to People, Planet and Profit,
All the wonderful things done till that benevolent moment.
For the life cherished, enriched, and inspired, from heart's back fit.
Not only recalling but hoping to achieve the targets placed for fulfilment.

Kids expecting a creamy decorated cake ready to slice and gobble.
The teenagers share the uproarious moment with closely-knit of the day;
The adults celebrate with family-knit environs fed by the offspring hobble,
Decently dressed, imploring the Mighty to protect until doomsday.

Oh, the wise even know not the date of arrival into this gorgeous world.
Toil daringly just to satiate the basics of food and thirst at a bare minimum,
Without ornate targets, but traverse with the risky tribulation by old and bold,
Though the poor and needy, yet benign to cherish rare ecstasy at maximum.

Though, 'B' day bash not dreamed of by millions around the resourceful globe:
Yet genuinely praise the Creator for the gift of life forgetting the trifling probe.

2.2

Inquisitive Initiation

Initiation – a religious ceremony conducted based on certain conventions:
A male believes a spiritual teacher as father, and the Vedas as mothers.
The Hindus, solemnize between 5 to 24 reflecting didactic obligations,
Mandated among these three – namely priests, warriors, and traders.

A ritual circumcision by aborigines, Egyptians, and tribes in African continent.
Jews and Muslims circumcise the males as a sign of a covenant with Almighty.
As rite of passage from babyhood to adolescence, yet others as grim, malignant.
Know not the reason, besides physical hygiene, and sanctity posed in the activity.

The rites of Baptism, Confirmation, and Eucharist form the Christian Initiation.
Baptism symbolizes the death of sin and union with Christ and the community.
Confirmation, seals an adolescent with the Holy Spirit by chrism oil consecration.
The Eucharist in the form of bread and wine signifies life's sustenance with Trinity.

Indeed, the rites and rituals hold value in the life of a devout adolescent.
Every being eventually realizes the transcendent in everything by calescent.

2.3

Magnificent Marriage

Marriage – a social event with plenty of merry-making around,
Celebrating with friends, relatives, and acquaintances, forgetting enmities.
Helping in decorating the venue with colorful lights and buntings to astound,
Thrilled faces with gaudiest clothes and ornaments, with designs like deities.

Past the days just agreed to tie knots for life with the unfamiliar girl or boy.
Seeking consent, trusting not the destiny of boons or yielding to the parents.
Assuring one another of support and sacrifice for futuristic and hopeful joy,
Enter into a new family for years, not recalling the home but as adherents.

God invented marriage and decided to fix the match from time immemorial.
Two become one to achieve a single objective, despite the shift of opinions.
Encounter strife in accomplishing the daily commitments like the imperial,
However, years pass by, keeping up the promises to live as companions.

Certified as a unit after the matrimonial oath amidst majestic carnival.
Whatever the situations pose, standing beside the partners like a subnival.

Better Together

2.4

Admirable Anniversary

Commemorating a special event that transpired previously, with gratitude,
Reminiscing the flashes of in-depth inspiration for relishing the impact.
Hoping to impersonate the values exposed with an aspiring attitude,
Celebrated with pomp, recapping the significance imposed with compact.

Initiated by the bourgeois ruling class, gifting the partner a silver crown,
Observing 25 years of marriage, and golden crowns upon 50 years of unison.
Starting with the paper year of marriage to the finest metal painted brown,
Signifying life from the fragility of objects to the robustness of union.

For each specialty, the types of stones and materials used symbolize tenacity,
Referring the longevity, by the precious stones as gifts to the living spouse.
Reveling the persistence in the marriage by the early positive audacity,
Dare to deviate from decimal to decimal, cherish the intimacy in the house.

Not only focus on the silver, gold, and diamond anniversary of marriage,
Being grateful to God for all stone birth anniversaries as a privilege.

2.5

Parting Party

Farewell, a bittersweet moment occurring in life, periodically,
Saying goodbye for the last in that phase of the rotational system.
Beholding 4 to 5 times during the pursuit of education, besides sporadically,
Based on the profession, either in the private or government firms, like an item.

The gurus consider everything an illusion that passes by, judged by the naked eye.
The professional experience, furtherance of skills and techs besides big money.
Hopping from one stage to another in search of expertise to settle as a pearl-eye.
Though part of life's survival process, leaving behind all types of sweet honey.

Fare-welling to numerous colleagues at various places and at eminent institutions,
Recalling a few with special background but with vivid memories of that person,
Either lousy or excellent or fun-loving pals, superiors, bosses in varied professions.
Impressed with indelible marks, imbibing values of both with impact reason.

The heartbreaking farewell confirmed not meeting anymore with each other.
Wow to modern technology, connecting nook and corner, not to bother.

CHAPTER 3

MASKED MASTERMINDS

3.1 Organic Ombudsman – The Organs
3.2 Seductive Secretaries – The Senses
3.3 Laminated Laboratory – The Limbs
3.4 Networking Notary – The Mind
3.5 Genuine Generator – The Heart

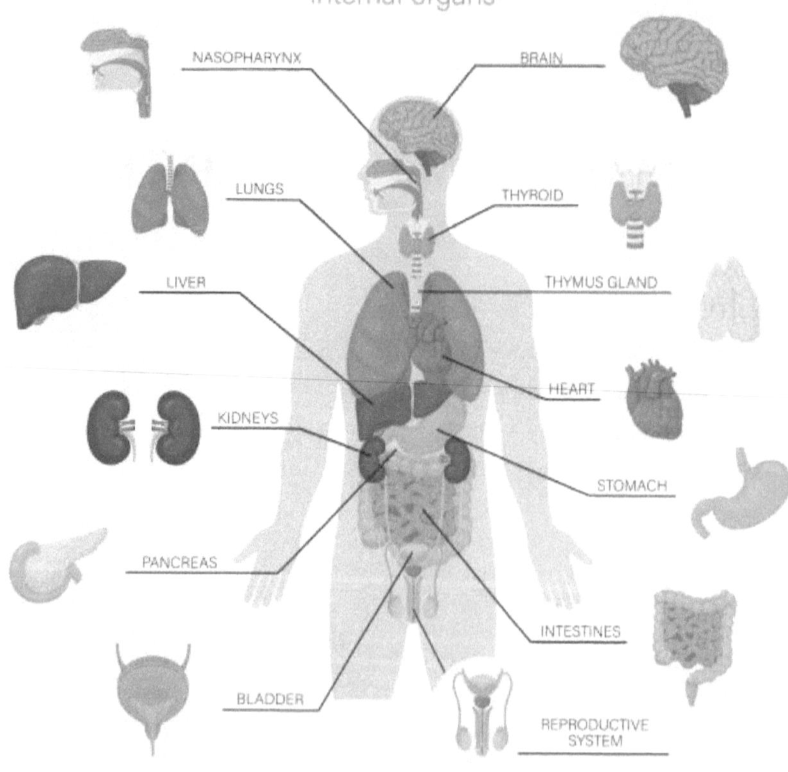
THE HUMAN BODY
Internal organs
NASOPHARYNX
BRAIN
LUNGS
THYROID
LIVER
THYMUS GLAND
HEART
KIDNEYS
STOMACH
PANCREAS
INTESTINES
BLADDER
REPRODUCTIVE SYSTEM

3.1

Organic Ombudsman – The Organs

Referred spontaneously, the internal organs sustain in a cyclic process.
Consciously as well as routinely carry forward the designed activity.
Stand by in solidarity with the battling, signaling the custodian to access,
Realizing tasks executed unassumed without smothering any stability.

Engraved behind the skin, the size, design, and color besides the health.
Awesomely depicting the electronic images to admire and appreciate.
Vitiate not the assigned works but execute diligently as great wealth,
Unless forced by unsolicited endeavors to maliciously depreciate.

Collaborating cordially amidst distinctions needs praiseworthy.
Generate the available nutrition according to the enabler's necessity.
Assailed with a subversive gratification exerted though unworthy,
Damaging and stripping off the doctor's proficiency and ability.

Placed as per the available capacity by the concern of the Almighty,
Monitor the magnanimity of the organs earnestly with undoubted honesty.

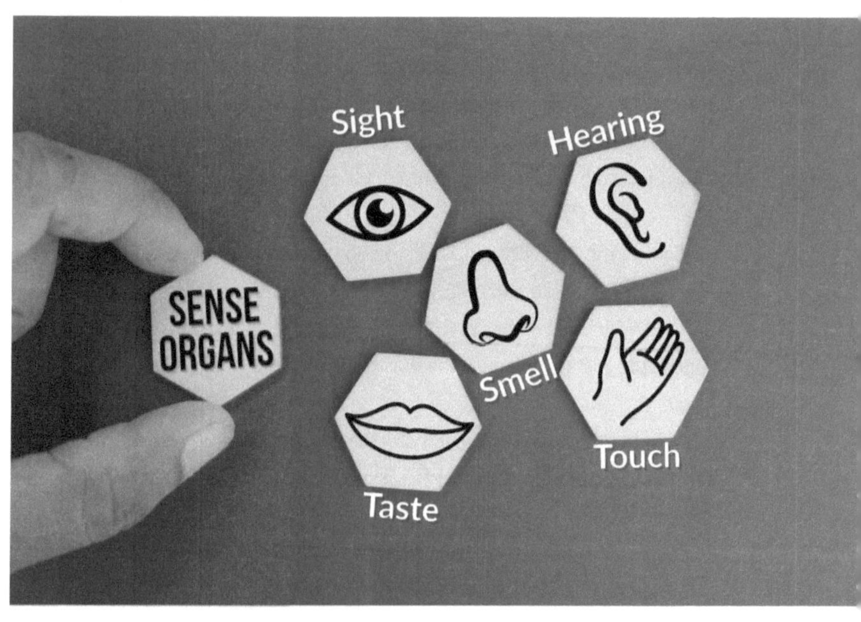
Sight
Hearing
SENSE
ORGANS
Smell
Touch
Taste

3.2

Seductive Secretaries – The Senses

Granted for, the precious and unique services rendered by day and night,
Not knowing the gravity of the situation, if, stopped functioning for a while.
Energizing and electrifying spontaneously through different actions at sights,
Though days pass on with mundane struggles and pain, the end leaves a smile.

Sensualize the others to peak by the chilling and titillating smear and touch!
Sensitize the moves and alert the steps toward unwanted and untoward motion.
Supply all empirical and existential experiences through the perceptive torch.
Elevate with treated aroma and fragrance and scare with petrifying devolution.

Satisfying the unending hunger and unquenchable thirst through the buds' taste,
Judging sternly before consuming the tastes: sweet, sour, salty, umami, and bitter.
Differentiate confidently to choose the best and discard the unappealing waste.
The senses act as the five elements of the universe to the body like a lighter.

Though the wise and literate opined twelve senses of experience leaven,
In fact, the five senses pave the way to delicious eleventh heaven.

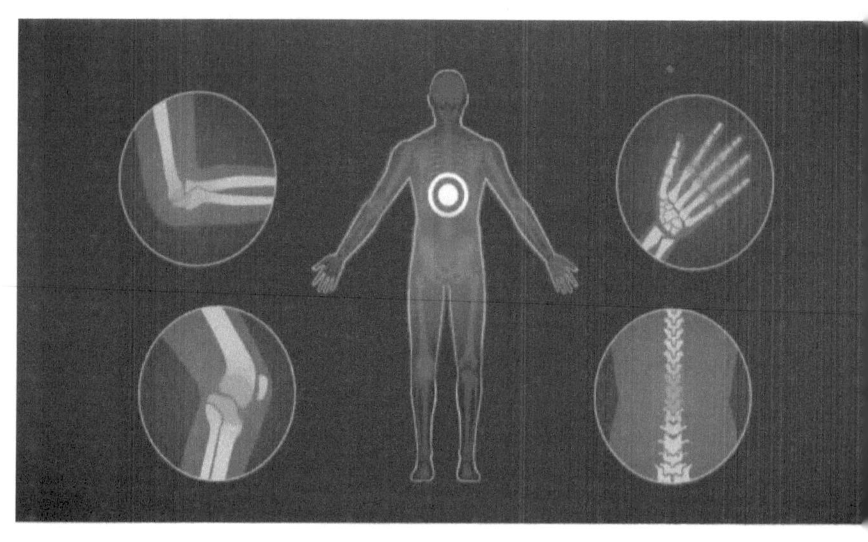

3.3

Laminated Laboratory – The Limbs

Enhancing the luminous elegance of the half-baked sensitive torso,
Energize the scrupulous trunk with dynamic roles in everyday sustenance.
Constructing completely by adding the delicate and complex limbs so,
From the initial movements expected of a humane body to the maintenance.

Bearing the whole weight placed above the downward elastic-like poles,
Elevate the upper body to view far-off scenic beauty by the glowing lights.
Freely enjoying the happiness generated from the radiant and gleaming holes,
Though discomfort in reaching the spot yet felt a lot of passionate insights.

Controlled by the engaged server behind the top corridor, the secured chamber,
Freely enacted and executed as per the spot requirement ordered and advised.
At times virulent, violent, and ferocious in execution but preferably in sober,
Satisfying the needs of every nut and bolt, the thirsting dependents raised.

Excluding the legs and hands, other limbs serve the dynamic roles as fixtured,
As per the designs interconnectedly and interdependently structured.

3.4

Networking Notary – The Mind

The Brain, physiologically referred to as the human mind, varies in function,
Structured the same in all and weighing approximately three pounds in adults.
Governing the activities of the entire body's dynamically in every friction,
Monitoring the heartbeats, respiration, generation, and secretion without faults.

Restless from the inception in the womb till reaching the ultimate destination,
Determining of success or failure, reward or punishment, rejection, or acceptance.
Satisfied not but craving more, realizing the impossibility of attaining ambition,
Intoxicated by vicious desires, aim at peculiar passions with reluctance.

Clapped by the spectators and well-wishers for the integrity built and exhibited,
Sought for the inherent treasure for the future career, targeted at with expectation.
Judged on the characters of a person based on the words and deeds prohibited,
Naughty in its thought process switching from time to time in desperation.

Wow, the human mind, gifted with multi-level phenomenon and genuineness,
Mysterious even for neuropsychologists, the behavior of the brain astuteness.

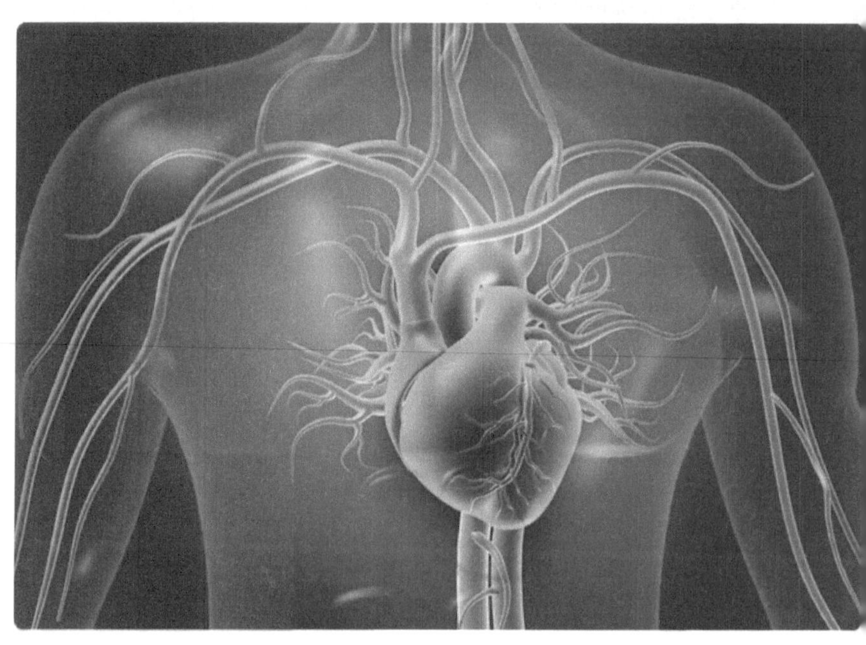

3.5

Genuine Generator – The Heart

Vital organ in the species keeps alive by flowing bloodline to the organs,
Pumping of blood by veins, with nutrition and oxygen, with tireless muscle.
A cumbersome workshop sleeps not a second in processing the inter-organs.
Hooray to the pump house owner to serve efficiently without a tussle.

Located between the lungs' cavity, with a pericardial fluid for protection.
Weighing from 230 to 340 grams, comprising 0.4.25% body capacity.
Boxed in 4 parts of 2 each atrium and ventricles, to evade any interruption.
In a rhythmic dynamism of the heart, pulsating 72 times per minute at intensity.

The heart executes a better role than the mind, as generally assumed by civilization.
The emotions of the breathing organism symbolized 'love' by the throbbing heart.
The cosmos orbits for love through a divergent sensory system of satisfaction.
Expressing gratification in words and deeds, the intimate experience of the smart.

The cherubim and seraphim exist, due to amorous heart, conveying filial affection.
Life lasts till the heartthrobs with a passion beyond the restriction of verification.

CHAPTER 4

MESMERIZING MEMORIES

4.1 Dared to Deviate – Wish against Wishes

4.2 First Flight – Sorrowful Skying

4.3 Grandeur Goa – Bachelors' Base Bashing

4.4 Routing against Rubrics – Innocent Ignorance

4.5 Emancipating Engagement – Experiment with Expelled

DARE TO DEVIATE

4.1

Dared to Deviate – Wish against Wishes

Unwillingly diverted from the core holy wish, realized later emptiness.
Reversing back to the subliminal pursuit that pestered not to rest.
Pondering on the cons and pros, discerned to stuff the hollowness,
To quench the soul's thirst headed forward to yield the best.

Reasonably tussled with the parent and the siblings, on futuristic effect.
Trusting in the divine power, the commotion erupted among the household.
Enlightened with harsh choices of pinning the roots, preferred any imperfect.
Stuck to the choice, firmly convinced by the desirous soul to behold.

Years traversed by, indoctrinating the holy wish into a fancy nomenclature,
Bothered not the rudiments of life experienced but concerned sporadically.
As, "the absence makes the heart grow fonder" – felt in an alien culture,
Questioned the destiny but realizing the power to change fate finally.

Though dared to deviate from the filial, instilled aspirations at the early stages,
Devoted a life contrarily from the natural process lived by sages bygone ages.

4.2

First Flight – Sorrowful Skying

Thought not traveling by flight in the near future, based on work and necessity.
Receiving a shockwave through a telegram of the sole breadwinner's departure,
With grief and remorse yet sprinted 300 km from the country to the metro city.
Embarked on the flight to tribute a dead corpse, trusting the pilot's stature.

Though amazed and wondered as the flight flew up toward the destination.
Yet the anguish of the untimely demise of Dad and the consequences thereafter.
Flabbergasted by the vibes, cherished not the Wright Brothers' great invention!
Soaked into melancholy of an existential philosophical reality of life and life later.

Reaching the halfway journey and rushed to the lounge to wait for the next flight.
Sporadically admired the creative innovation of the mortals in designed fixtures.
As the call echoed for further journey, proceeded to a seat at the sober light.
The scenic earth at the sunset, admired the creator for the marvelous features.

Forget not the journey from BBI to HYD and HYD to MAA without glee,
Rarely relish the fatiguing journeys, the intrusion of the cloudy sky with a plea.

4.3

Grandeur Goa – Bachelors' Base Bashing

The picturesque seashores of the Arabian Sea engulfing the Goan coast,
Enticed by the renowned beaches and the remnants of the Portuguese legacy,
Fortunate to visit the grandeur of Goa and enriched with party toast.
Touched by Portuguese ethnicity lingering in the Goan's life and delicacy.

The enthralling archaeological site of Bom Jesu Basilica amidst the tourists,
The deep-sea trips on motorized boats titillate both mind and body apart, compare.
The enchanting carnivals celebrating the moments of life with amorists.
The Mandovi and Zuari rivers stand as Goa's agriculture industry and opera share.

Wondered at the decorated and orderly designed bottles sealed with fizzy wine,
Enjoyed a lot the hot as well as frosted booze and a pippy-crispy fish dish.
Winked at the semi-steamed fleshly stuff of garlands out of farm-grown swine,
Purchased colorfully engraved sketch of tops and shorts with cheaply lavish.

The 7 months sojourn in Goa's southern region exposed the arts and culture,
Christianizing the state as "God's own swimming pool" for its magical nature.

4.4

Routing against Rubrics – Innocent Ignorance

Rubrics of the traditions set forth a framework for objective decisions.
Smoothen the life of individuals and organizations, avoiding the risk of conflicts.
Focusing on appropriate and cordial relationships in all interactions and impositions,
Reprimanding the vitiations, to adhere to the guidelines, in order to prevent derelicts.

Ignorance, though bliss, but knowledge – power! ignored due to oblivious admiration.
In the garden of strengths, ignorance as such, weeded out to adopt virtuous valor.
Purity without intellect fails at the root of the characters, imbibed with determination.
Like the fight amid the mongoose and snake, finally power overwhelms the frail bailor.

Willful pride contradicted the valuable motion, but without gaining any, bereft at heart.
Pleasured in advocating hurtful executions, but later realizing the sadistic ventures.
Crewed physically, engineered mentally, and tagged the position with empty art,
With anxious and atrocious endeavors, effortlessly seeking gratification like vultures.

Though soothing to the feelings and to the senses but disturbed the conscience.
Frankly confess whatever restricts the human tendencies, desires for an ebullience.

4.5

Emancipating Engagement – Experiment with Expelled

Venturous, audacious, and daring to acquire momentum of the targets.
Traveled at 21 to accumulate spiritual strength from the marginally managed,
Known as the "City of Joy – Kolkata," noticed the suffering around life begets.
Served in the hospices of the MCs, in caring for the disadvantaged.

Exposure among the lepers, triggered the horrifying scenes with heavy heartbeats.
Despite of the petrifying smell triggering the brain cells and reducing the intake.
Searched for the needy with ID cards along with medicines, at swift beats.
Nursed the sick and insane wherever found, not bothering for a break.

Sojourned in an asylum to foster the mentally retarded by bathing and dressing.
With extra courage to execute a motherly act never performed in the earlier stage.
Dealing with the ragpickers, notoriously sparkling, but empowered with caressing.
Coupled with physical and a psychological caliber rendering in the orphanage.

The sojourn with emotionally, physically, cerebrally, and socially deprived,
Enriched life and counting down the blessings with gratitude for not contrived.

CHAPTER 5

NURTURING NATURE

5.1 The Soothing Spring
5.2 The Scorching Summer
5.3 The Rejuvenating Rain
5.4 The Attractive Autumn
5.5 The Whimsical Winter

5.1

The Soothing Spring

After a tediousness due to the earth tilts, emerges the soulful spring,
Invigorating the environs with new and freshened fragrances around.
Observing festivals throughout the globe, identifying God's blessing,
Embracing the foliage across the dwelling by capturing the sight beyond.

From mid-February to April end, with periodic showers and winds,
Occasionally rippling with depression swelled from deep to sandy bosom.
Within titillating feelings and emotions, radiating to the surrounding kinds,
Signaling the newness, surpassing beyond limits like a soothing blossom.

Observed with pomp and valor, the traditional feasts and memorials,
Such as Panchami, Ugadi, Holi, Rama Navami, Vishu, Bihu, Baisakhi,
Tamil New Year, and the great mysteries of Lord Jesus Christ's apparitions,
Personifying the nature to the events around with unintentional freaky.

Valuing the temperateness generated from this reassuring moment around,
Even though global warming proliferates, marking its brand all around.

5.2

The Scorching Summer

Invading with ferocity, bothered least to show mercy even to the upright.
Positioning the planet like the eagle at its prey, with a relentless look,
Making days longer and nights shorter, though hours parallel with the light.
Dipping rigor by relaxing the intellectual machine, even from a fascinating book.

Regardless of its nature, abundantly provides different types of fruits at its rifts,
Ranging from small berries to huge watery fruits, and from juicy to fiber nuts,
Quenching the throats and the sensing palettes to taste nature's lavish gifts.
Though hard at heart, yet sensitive towards humankind by defending from ruts.

Though atrocious at attitude, rejuvenate the site with revitalizing evenings,
Harbingering the fortune to crisscross the periodic recurrent cruelties.
Nevertheless, testing the perseverance of the impatient fellow beings,
Yet appreciate the civic attitude to worship Gods in a couple of festivities.

Craved by the children for a gathering with the kith and kin in a distant land,
Oh, dear Summer, making things memorable even for a brand.

5.3

The Rejuvenating Rain

Felt from June to August, expected as per climatic condition,
Petitioning the Almighty to safeguard the mass for future posterity.
Offspring life along with elements of the universe, despite of devastation,
Longing for ardently by the farmers to load the waterbodies for prosperity.

Organisms expect bountiful showers to escape the scorching heat and aridity.
Enriched by the rain, both humanoid and animal kingdoms from desiccation.
Warning patients prone to rain-born ailments not to loiter by imposing rigidity,
To avoid untoward skidding due to wetness besides unhealthy hypertension.

Marked by deafening thunder storms, lightning, and evil-seized gales,
Wetting as usual routine along with executing the envisioned aspirations.
Disrupt the slated plans by disheartening contenders exuberate hearty hales,
Dislocate ennui even in enthusiasts as its nature driving into dull situations.

Adoring Raksha Bandhan and Janmashtami by the faithful at fitting locations,
Hunting for fancy umbrellas adjacent as a rescuer of the conditions.

5.4

The Attractive Autumn

Hey, falling before winter, triggering the weather by hypnotizing charm,
Expediency for the farmers to harvest most of the crops along with berries.
Venture with veg – carrots, beets, cabbage, cauliflower, and beans in the arm,
Surge into bazaar with salivating fruits along with rare figs and cherries.

Feasted Navratri, Durga Puja, Diwali, Shard Purnima with pompadour,
Grateful to the creator for the benevolence bestowed abundantly.
Soberly pleasurable environment of the season in the surrounding odor,
Unique the season because of succor even the bottom pyramid ardently.

Touring with kith and kin to charming zones, both picturesque and mystic,
Lack of rain, the trees wither, and the foliage, but the gorgeous spots enthrall.
The dye of the flora turns every greenery yellow, making the scene fantastic,
Migrating to newer sites and reptiles store food for untoward nature's call.

Oh, the splendor of autumn refreshing a new biosphere exhibiting candidly,
Equinox phase craved even by the terrorists, blunting acts splendidly.

5.5

The Whimsical Winter

Greeneries with immaculate flora and dense foliage, with a soothing destination,
Entrancing aroma from the blossoms with tickling hues of benevolent nature,
Caressed from Dec. to Feb, tying a knot between two years of expansion,
Attired with woolen warm clothes, heralding biting cold with icy temperature.

Fill the shops with apples, pomegranates, kiwi, strawberry, and mulberry,
Herding the market with turnips, radishes, collard, spinach, beans, and peas,
Enticing the consumers to taste of its worth, invested as part of life's merry,
Feasting of Christmas, Lohri, Pongal, and Sankranti by seeking peace.

Pretty weather, even slogging for hours in the field, in the offices, or at home,
Fresh at the end of the labor, to chill out with colleagues of close-knit,
Turning heavenly leisureliness into glum hellishness due to nature's dome,
Finally, favors importance only for humans, not nature as part of the unit.

Gone the enmity created by the onslaught of words but in quest of collaboration,
Yearned for the time for fun-loving picnics with the like-minded association.

CHAPTER 6

PASSIONATE PROFESSIONS

6.1 Adorable Actors and Actresses
6.2 Benevolent Businessman
6.3 Deified Doctor
6.4 Fabulous Farmers
6.5 Jet Journeying Journalist
6.6 Admonishing Advocates
6.7 Power-Positioned Politician
6.8 Sophisticated Scientist
6.9 Superheroes Soldiers
6.10 Sanctifying Sanitationists

6.1

Adorable Actors and Actresses

Coveted career, required passion coupled with special skills and talents.
Respectable name, fame, and money along with the joy of performing.
Recognition by the public folk, big bucks if logged, stylized patents.
Devoted time perfecting from an amateur to master blast, zooming.

Disputed at sorting out reality of life in society with added imagination,
Depicted with flowery dialogs, harsh chiding, and crude consequences,
Engrossing in the play-acting, with mind and heart in the rotation,
Grasping the climax with intuitions, triggered by the scenic occurrences.

Influencing to succumb to the reality lived, like the cloaked opium.
The heroes and heroines appear fancily on the screen after impersonating.
The ethical, mythical, and mimic behaviors come across in life's atrium.
Involved rapturously as though seen the self-caricatured role in the acting.

Indeed, making even the stony-hearted choice to change based on chance.
Even a pauper hits at a fortune if prospects knock on the screen trance.

6.2

Benevolent Businessman

Workaholic, especially at the executive level as a producer, industrialist,
Seller, trader, etc., dealing with all types of customers for financial gain,
Satisfying the aspired inspirations in acquiring a position in the fame list.
Serving, sustaining and creating livelihood for many to maintain.

Defined as an enterprising entity engaged in lucrative activities:
Under professional production and service, tagging as profitable venture,
Like the bees haunting from morning until late evening parties,
Focused on Money, 'Kaasu,' 'Duttu,' and 'Rupiah' without a puncture.

The apt quality of an efficacious business driving into a bizarre pitch.
With experience booms business prosperity at every dealing and agreement.
Working smartly and inspiration on firmness to cast out the lazy witch.
Rejuvenating the crewmembers raises the toast beyond the entertainment.

'Finance is the blood' of businesses to transfuse the blood to different portions
Risk-taking and robust techno-savvy system for future market competitions.

6.3

Deified Doctor

The Doctor, the most important and lifesaving person in society,
Supporting the infirm, young, and old, struggling with health hazards.
Saving from diseases and symptoms for which the ailing deifies with piety,
Hope in every touch, experience the unknown power with learned wizards.

A sloka states, "Doctors are brothers of the 'Yama Raj.' The Satan snatches:
The life of people, but the doctors not only life but also the wealth."
The ability of human being to comprehend the body anatomy and stitches;
Marvel mystery when medicine non-cooperates, yet the patient regains health.

Millions become doctors for several reasons including as dedicated medics.
In the countries where poverty, war, and political turmoil prevail rampantly.
God performs miracles every day, but also the doctors, in all the clinics.
Replacing the creator, the healthcare providers serve the public constantly.

Placing this noble profession among the elite and honorable in society,
Because of the knowledge and wisdom in treating the infirm with piety.

6.4

Fabulous Farmers

Farmers, the backbone of a society, regardless of color, creed and location.
Slogging to fill our stomachs periodically with the basic cooked food item.
Not only for self-ingestion of the products but also for others' consumption.
Shouldering the task of feeding millions of people in a regular system.

For the munificence of the humanity, the trees bear fruits, the river flows,
The cows provide milk; if so, for the benefit of all, sacrifice our bodies.
Indeed, in showcasing, the farmers toil the earth with updated new plows.
Schemes for the farmers' benefit, required support from the civic bodies.

Salute them for providing enough food to humanity for existence.
Elevating life from the scarcity of food causing hunger and starvation.
Due to the nature's benevolence, adore it spontaneously for sustenance.
Siding luxury, but honor the Mother Earth to avoid wrath and deprivation!

Holding a vital obligation for a country to live in peace and harmony.
Ensuring a prosperous future though looked very fatigue and monotony.

6.5

Jet Journeying Journalist

Motivated by a passionate love towards Earth and the living creature,
To enlighten the reality without coding much, to the craving humanity.
Furnishing the information with facts and figures meticulously that nurture,
The population for tingling and beguiling news occurring in far-off vicinity.

With an adventurous attitude, traverses to unfamiliar zones to check reality,
Reporting based on the "seeing is believing", to the observers and audience.
Accompanied by a color mic, to live telecast to the spectators with morality,
Expecting not recognition but focused only on collecting evidence.

Confronting tough situations, even lathi charges in grave circumstances.
Getting mysterious calls if the reports upset any lived beliefs, sentiments,
Creeds, etc., but irrespective of such weird, and frightening occurrences,
Persist in endeavors with passion burning within for common commitments.

To endow reality to the populace at regular intervals signals the untoward,
Though fetches profits for life, but mitigates in opening the incidents forward.

6.6

Admonishing Advocates

Presents and argues on behalf of another in defending from legal aberration,
Known in other way as advocate, barrister, solicitor, attorney, and prosecutor.
Argue on behalf with a black coat, white shirt, and a tie-band with preparation,
Debating logically the motions placed in the proceeding by the chair solicitor.

With an expert educational endeavor in the field and enrolling in the bar council,
Shoulder as legal representative either for a fee or for a kind for the advocation.
Arguing either way, along with references to past verdicts and law with codicil,
Settle the trials and tribulations of economic, mental, and physical suffocation.

Name and fame for defending clients' innocence and guilt with facts and figures,
Mesmerizing the spectators with 'Wah' feelings, for proving the judgment chairs.
With precise conviction, discuss the issue seeking fruition in favor of the adjures,
Opportune by a difference in society to establish justice and peace in pairs.

Though challenging, the prospect sets into professional career and a reward,
Aptly amending the conflict situations while aware of the cases in laggard.

HAMARA
NETA
JINDABAD

6.7

Power-Positioned Politician

Involves in the governance of civic, including healthcare, education,
Welfare, and the distribution of responsibility among the governing members.
Supervise the application of policies, regulations, and schemes in the location,
Intended to gain popularity among the people and mitigating flaws by cybers.

In ancient civilization, people gathered in forums to discuss the issues of life.
Now, evolved a system of local to global governance due to interrelatedness.
Civility probed into networking mechanisms, seeking cooperation in all strife,
Emerging into a new consciousness in society for upholding righteousness.

Though politically identify with Robinhood characteristics in the endeavors,
Demonstrate hooliganism in executing charity for the benefit of constituents.
Breach in fulfilling selfish motives, seizing under control dummy devours.
Display selflessness and justice, deceptively promise amenities to the residents.

No fixed time of duty and responsibility but claim 24x7 in serving the public.
Indeed, not much for family but for society with noble thoughts of prolific.

6.8

Sophisticated Scientist

Thrilled in figuring out strange and unique features in natural phenomena,
Venturing into the systematic search for strings of evidence and corroboration.
Exploring the source and reaction, and cause and effect in a specific arena,
Engrossed for hours in the intellectual sphere, not focusing on physical satiation.

Unraveling the mysteries of nature and its magnificent power for advancement,
Protecting life through experiments, devising solutions for alleviating suffering.
Attaining bliss for intelligentsia at the triumph of inventions for enrichment,
Drawn by enigmatic entities, distinguish from other populace in the maneuvering.

Venture into the triple bottom: 'people, planet, and profit,' upgrading collectively,
Focusing on not only existing generations but also of future descendants.
As desired peace, progress, plenty, and prosperity in endeavors instinctively,
But target the results benefiting a multitude of ages along with confidants.

Traverse into 'mysterious features' exposing reliable prospects to civilization,
Work hard with a mission of 'dedication,' emancipating at best completion.

6.9

Superheroes Soldiers

Pledged life to safeguard the nation from internal and external powers.
With bravery, stand erect-like stupas at the borders, showcasing valor.
Swift to forward for the reverential love of motherland among the bowers,
Soldiers – the assets of a country holding pride on assiduousness of armor.

Encompassed by service, in defense of the snares of the foes,
Despite hurdles, considering the aspect of duty as an innate merit.
No other duty match with such passion, daring even the floes,
Focused on preserving safety by blocking intruders, even the ifrit.

With will and resilience in an extraordinary way, confronting dangers,
Pirouette the vicinity to ambush the trespassing militants in dare.
Like speediest Cheetahs, and strongest elephants in ensnaring the avengers,
Endure the exotic climates just for the dignity of Mother Earth's care.

Salute the souls for inculcating values in robust manner in emergencies,
Sustaining the honored professions, slogging under bizarre exigencies.

Sanctifying Sanitationists

Uphold hygiene without devaluing the service rendered to the population,
Committed despite the rain and wind, scorching heat, and shivery freezing.
Spruce up the town by cleaning and discarding putrefying garbage collection.
Protect the city from being a rotten junkyard without creating a wheezing.

Electricians vivify the streets with flashing lights, turning the night into day.
Defeating the mountaineers but proving with knack descendants of apes.
Stabilizing power by chipping and trimming the hasty trees on the roadway.
Thwart off the complaints and pacify the disgruntled residents' rapes.

Safeguard the source of life – 'water' for all types of physical fitness.
For every living organism's occupational survival and bodily satisfaction.
The plumbers dedicatedly supply water sources intermittently with fairness.
Expecting a yearly allowance from the beneficiaries for the servitor action,

Slog dedicatedly daily for a low wage but essential for the city's health.
Exposed to dangerous sicknesses, but just to survive, not for wealth.

CHAPTER 7

PSYCHOSOMATIC SENSATIONS

7.1

The Unimaginable Imagination

Surpassing the restricted boundaries inflicted by the capricious souls,
Cancerous in nature; not sparing age, so-called caste, color, and creed;
With utter perseverance, minds of ardent achievers for fame from soles,
Causing the empty vessels' unquenchable desires and vicious greed.

Brilliant inventions and mind-boggling discoveries the souls cherish,
Either pondering on hours or triggered with a friction of a second.
Smothering the situation with solid and liquid stuff to relish,
Making moments experience in the minds of the ambitious brand.

Plot with the horrific embodiment of compassion and disposition,
Not realizing its unexpected vengeance in the deserted location.
Indoctrinating the enchanting and mesmerizing notation,
Unknowingly inserting volumes to control the untoward situation.

Behaves like a legitimate child, though deserves all the legatee rights,
Yet placed behind the picturesque scene not traced by the naked sights.

7.2

Expect the Unexpected!

Congregated ardently to unfurl the nation's flag on a cloudy, snooty,
A monstrous gale ventured, baffling everyone, run hither thither.
Disgusted by the enigmatic nature, exhibited naughty and haughty,
Waited for hours to upheave the national tricolor in a bit of bother.

As usual, passed the sweltering summer day with a sizzling, vivid Sun.
Organized a haunting farewell evening to the seniors on the open ground,
Enthusiastically assembled with a variety of entertainment for great fun,
Sudden downpouring the sky, leaving the arena feebly dumbfounded.

A month-long arrangement for the memorable annual convocation,
Making the academic nitty-gritty for executing efficiently and faultlessly,
Just cherishing the hard work of the graduates' educational completion,
There popped up the harbinger monsoon, embarrassing all rebelliously.

Intended, deliberated, arranged, and finally hoped to execute the best,
Not contemplating the mercy of elegant nature's succor with full of zest.

7.3

Carefronting Conflicts

The conflicts, severe or trivial, in usual affairs of prevalent notion,
Occurs at home, in the workplace, at the market, and in betting.
Out of irritation, out of infatuation, or out of defiance based on option,
Due to limited gifts by the Almighty or by the nature of the setting.

An expression topsy-turvy the circumstances into indelible collision,
Altering know-how into daunting incidences amidst the adorable buddy.
Accusatory of others, not trusting or superfluous in intimating compassion,
Getting across the views denotes the confrontation of glowed-up rowdy.

In carefrontation, love dominates the center of attraction through dialog,
Softened in the tough discourse to persuade the golly behind the clash.
Deletion of toxic in the affiliation built-in without retaining a log,
Sustains the carefrontation to the sinister motive mates wait for a bash.

Conflicts emerge and vanish on the surface for survival and sustenance,
But confrontations cohabit the genera for preservation and maintenance.

TOASTMASTERS
INTERNATIONAL

7.4

Trustworthy Toastmasters

Debating for clarity and confidence, in judging the regular endeavors.
Boosting and firmly solving with connections; the decisions projected.
Ad hoc reactions from the pals, with the arguments for pursuing favors,
Marching with resolutions justified by prior experience implemented.

Genuine comradeship depends on trustworthiness and faithfulness,
The relationships portray the gap between the worthy and the unworthy.
Mutual justice, forgiveness, and the ability to take risks of courageousness,
The sacrificial love without any fear or resentment, orienting noteworthy.

Supplementing aspirants for utilizing the skills to improve the process.
Inaugurating a venture into untraversed frontiers of occupational extends.
Gather mosses through experimentation and intruding into new accesses,
A Toastmaster signifies in demonstrating techniques without pretends.

Trustworthy Toastmasters, comrades, friends, and mates support mutually,
Without any formalities in enhancing the lifestyle in every sphere cordially.

7.5

Nauseating Nicknames

Noted diversely, such as the quality of an individual or an incident.
Analogy or attributes, on the size, color, or appearance of the thespian.
Of animals or associations, denoting a prevalent charisma or style intended,
Creative rhyme by the prefix or suffix to a tag, or abbrev of a name, utopian.

Triggering hate between folks belonging to two distinct realms or a doctrine,
Unifying two divergent groups to combat the third party's undue dominance,
Assisting a role of power in the clusters tormented by derisive stuff like urine,
Realizing the dependence with bunches, yielding not to derogative prominence.

Refusing to participate in the pal's persevering endeavors out of desperation.
Parting due to incongruous moniker baptized by the chum's ordinance imposed.
For attesting erroneously, improvise the weird charm into esteemed arrogation.
Controvert the sobriquet ascribed deficiently beyond the acceptance proposed.

If the epithet adds value to the personality of a person, hilariously acclimatized.
But wait to discard and reverse the alias with a novelty, avoiding stigmatization.

CHAPTER 8

REJUVENATING RELATIONSHIPS

8.1

Magnanimous Mother

Apart from exposing this mesmerizing world and feeling for all now,
Molded this offspring, besides kindhearted to the poor in a dire empathy,
Standing steady like an ornate monument, even future generations bow,
Compromised not on the discipline, yet occasionally in slight sympathy.

Simple philosophy, hope-filled theology, easing troubles more practical,
Then the robotic brain trained in labs, though undoubtedly convincible,
Constantly inspiring from emotive examples, although beyond hypothetical,
A preamble for preparing for life's journey meaningful and sensible.

Gratitude-filled gracious heart, devotedly reminisced the people of kindness,
Stop not though troubled by inflation and deflation in the economic paucity,
Blathering away from the existential system due to capable strictness,
Remaining always a genuine visionary with serenity as well as tranquility.

Exhibited stupendous, fabulous, and extraordinary affection to all, Oh Dear!
Thanks for wonderful life beyond any verbal expression, "My Mother."

8.2

Fervent Father

The breadwinner of the growing-up children and spouse, meekly laboring,
Besides sufficing boarding and lodging, clothing, and social obligations,
Relying on farming, along with shepherding, and biweekly brokering,
Earned the livelihood without surreptitious covert or wicked inclinations.

Frequented the fair markets on Wednesdays and Fridays with great ambitions,
Longed for the return to munch other than the homemade cereals and snacks,
Busy with classes the whole day, waiting for the dad with great expectations,
Came inebriated or fatigued but with a good amount in the inner packs.

A simple, emanated hard work, and advised wisely only in dire necessity,
With reverential fear honored to the brim for the steadfast love in fathering,
Trudged with the goal of developing the future generation's wished capacity,
But disheartened with the way life turned into familial and social hurling.

As stated, anything poisonous consumed in abundance for benevolence,
Addicted to alcoholism, deserted the kith and kin to the eternal inheritance.

The most important things in life
are not things...

8.3

Sentimental Sisters

Blessed or not, amidst four sisters of honesty and ardent bravery,
Though not accomplished anything extraordinary, or outstanding.
Struggled with existing means, neither in greed nor in snoozed slavery,
Indebted to the Mighty, pursuing refuge in 'HIS' extravagance, holding.

The oldest, traversed far-flung boundaries for adequate sustenance,
The second sweats with the land for survival, quenching manual labor.
The third, though qualified for subsistence, slogs for maintenance,
The last, petted by all, makes a modest homemaker in the spouse's favor.

Longed for bounteous prosperity at the doorjambs with their spouse,
Destiny exhibits as per its whims and fans not of individual's ambition.
Blaming the mother for prejudice and favoritism, tending ambiguous,
Not commenting more, it's part of life everyone realizes this notion.

These four pillars resemble the four directions, with specified aspirations,
Adding values to each one's expectations through existential limitations.

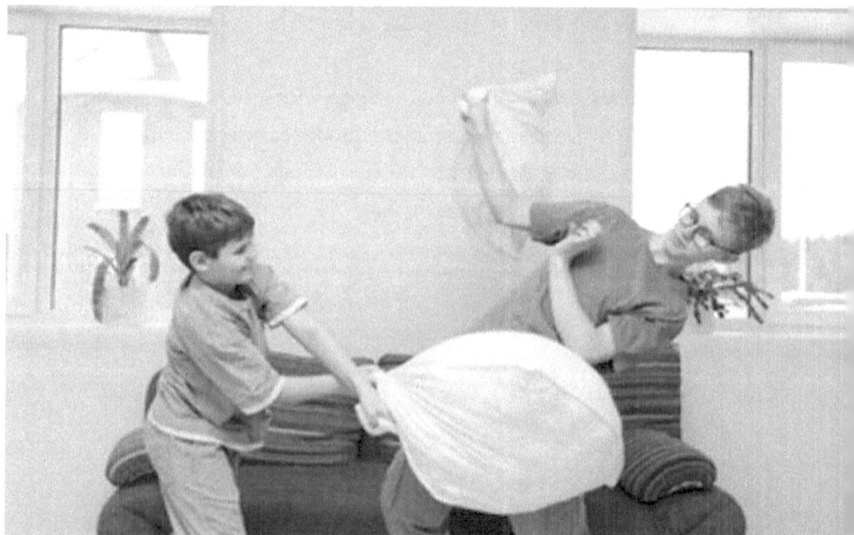

8.4

Bothersome Brothers

Boned with two younger buddies of different temperaments and stature,
Worthy, yet with the personality blended with North Pole and South Pole.
Though grew up under the military regime, shaping a luminous future.
Gawkily distorted after an oversight, handing over for a conscientious role.

The sassy elder-younger grabbed the fortune to pursue a cozy education,
Preyed to economic scarcity, dropping behind furtherance of opportunity.
Resumed school, troubled by instigated torments to the wedded sibling,
Risked career, left home in search of future, not realizing the lot in vanity.

The younger young, not rapt in treasuring wisdom for a brighter radiance,
Accomplished high schooling by closing the books and opening no longer.
Wandered for survival but landed back blank without a ray of assurance,
Forced by self-catastrophe, trudges with the domestic beasts as a loner.

With pitiable pursuit, but not ignoring the battles and inevitable adversities,
Though not often, stretching hands and head in alleviating the difficulties.

8.5

Gifted Grandchildren

Of the 6 children's progeny of 15, a range from 30 to 5 years span
7 perfect numbers of ingenious boys with creativity and practicality
8 propitious numbers of girls with divinity and infinity not to scan.
Grown by leaps and bounds in the conventional yet free spirituality.

Spread far and wide, intimately knit the juveniles in the granny's cuddle.
Indoctrinated values enduring to confront adversity of mysterious flashes.
Hoping to construct a prospect undetermined beyond the mortal's handle.
Relishing life, despite the constraints and opportunities accessed in lashes.

Fostered faith in pursuing and promoting peace to develop a novel humanity.
Imploring the Supreme to shield the buds from the clutches of antagonists.
Deliberately or by accident penetrating the fidelity; for the reward of serenity
Illusions of the earth entice and assault the recalcitrant as an assured atheist.

Persuading ever obligated to the altruism of the unreserved ultimate Divinity.
Without opacities, Granny aspires to grandchildren's posterity in a fraternity.

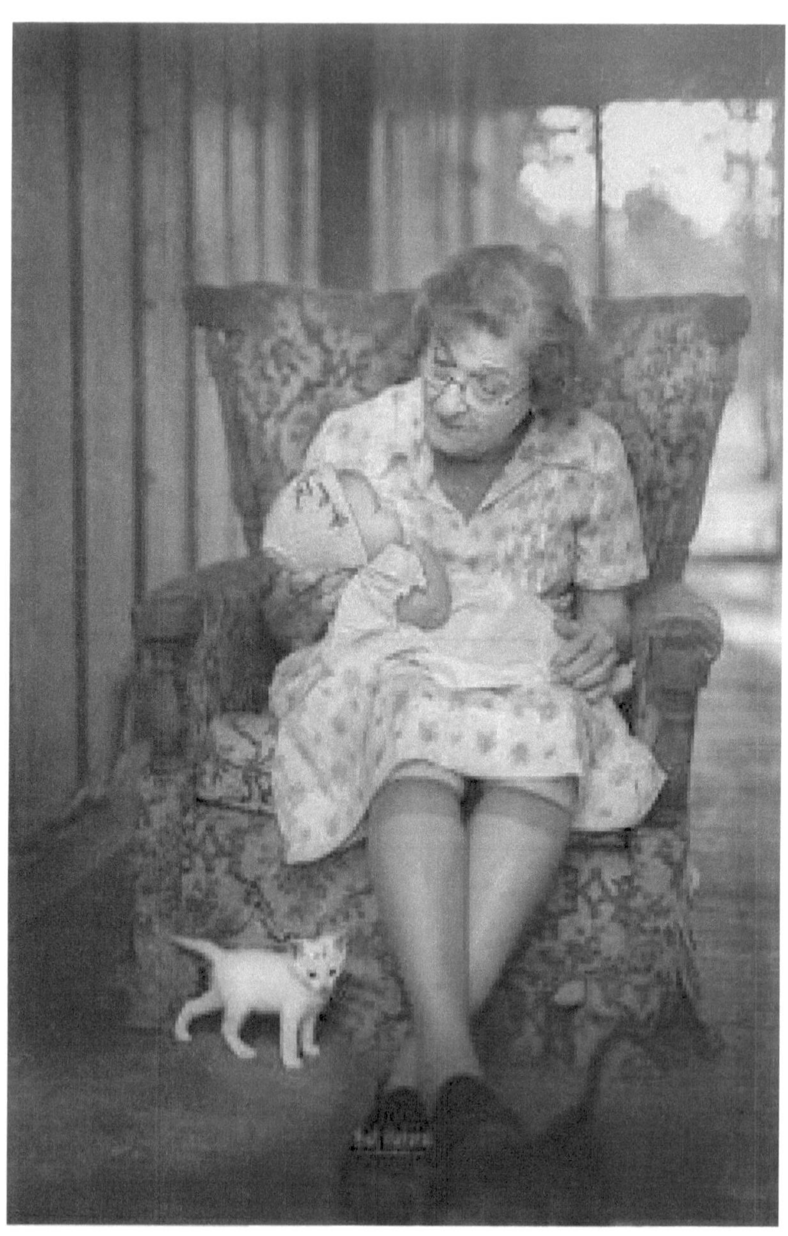

8.6

Gracious Grandparents

Grandparents, senior in the family, affectionate all times, tentatively serious
Filled with facts and wisdom invariably practical in executing deliberation.
Well-informed about the neighbors pretending unknown but bit mischievous.
Expert in rumors if not, adored by anyone even with witty aberration.

More caring, respected unlike other family members for the superior attitude
As the angels, with extra pampering the youngsters with ethical nurturing.
Play like vitamins to grow into a wonderful person with granny similitude.
Bridge the gap between the generations through magical manuring.

Generous to the grandchildren to have extreme fun and frolic for expertise.
Carefronted in upbringing the offspring parented before Pearl Jubilee's party.
Handle the family disputes with carefrontation before boiling into spamvertise.
Safeguarding the family tradition to pass on as potentially future property.

Grandparents Day celebrated to remember fondly the time spent on laps.
But ignored by most due to sophisticated lifestyle creating unfamiliar gaps.

8.7

Buckled Buddies

Evoking the bygone days, shoved, and yanked in the exhilarated aura.
Without the comrades, drawn-out days, snappier nights, dreary body
Infused by the chums' mind to implement astute deeds in open flora.
Aid for a righteous cause even flaming fingers not bothering the bloody

Shared and spared a lot out of care, heroically wrestled with, out of the loop.
On the riverbed, smeared with muddy glue, luxuriated the baffling Sunlight.
Played weird games under the water squeezing with our torso during a hop.
Bathed under pumped water in nudity without any inhibition in the daylight.

Sat in stillness by hearting lessons and clearing doubts from the pals' intuition.
Confronted logically the clairvoyance proposed by the comrades in the debate.
Argued on favorite celebrities and showcased the caliber of onerous imitation.
Incorporated girls in the squad to fill the number for action in a teenage senate.

Met rarely with diverse occupations, split by miles without any secret motive.
But cluster in WhatsApp, yet inaudible of the Buddies' gullible objective

8.8

Tenacious Teacher

Extreme elegance in letters with unique in the assertion of language,
The deeds imprinted in the pupils' passionate and resolute endeavors.
Spick and span, hale and hearty, despite undesirable progress in age,
Affectionate heart with the sternness of peeking lingers in lit favors.

Utter awe for the teacher boosted interest in the lessons tutored.
Indeed, coupled with a dedication for making better creatures.
Wished not a call, not for applause but for whips due to less scored.
Instilling the target on all attendees' gurus of the unfathomable futures.

Source of ideas ignited equally through explicitly profound illustrations,
Recalling the ecstatic reminiscences traversed in, then fervent aspirants
Never sighted, leaving the proficiency center with indefinite ambitions
Reviving the golden memories, infusing sense in present postulants.

Vanished from the scene yet loitering fondly in the effective decisions,
Of the hopefuls lavishly cherishing the unconditional life dedications.

8.9

Cordial Comrades

"Friendship is the melody and fragrance to life," stated wonderfully.
Such phrases haunt the heart and mind as though traveling on Everest.
However, the other defaults intentionally or not, accept the fault willfully.
Because either inhibition or restriction shut the conversation of the nearest

Friends in abundance at a time of interminable fame and profuse prosperity
But a few around irrespective of economic paucity and socially insecure
Lavishly utilized the notoriety and accomplishments ascribed to posterity.
Not even hinted, due to restricted limitedness in the sophisticated obscure

A true friend carefronts and confronts in moments of inappropriateness.
Realizing the sourness created by unpleasant interactions yet with serenity.
Not bothered by the judgmental consequences of the efficient effectiveness
Solely succoring as before in all the interrelations with slight modernity.

Although name, fame, and achievements vanish with the shifting wind.
Exists forever friendship, despite mysterious famine and plague, not kind.

8.10

Fascinating First Fall

Debated the topic from timeworn on 'First fall' or "love at first sight".
Reminding the contention even as ages passed by in classical literature.
About Romeo and Juliet – portrayed in the play by W.S. as a love plight.
Rendering young to realize the shadows that prevent inner acupuncture.

Expressed not in words the tickling triggers enraptured in the empty hotpot.
Fused with shyness, never exhibited by any form of visible communication.
But controlled the volcanic desires and emotions due to parents' despot!
Lacked a basic sense of discerning whether a true love or infatuation.

As adolescence, pondered on ambitions by retracting biological recreation.
Flew to strange terrain deserting kith and kin and not expressing first love.
Eclipsed by a vision, departed the own land, steered on to the destination.
Hoped to meet face to face but never, at least to pacify the soul's trove!

'First Love' emotions haunted at random referring to life's existence.
Failed to execute in this birth, for opting life of spiritual sustenance.

CHAPTER 9

UNIQUENESS OF THE UNIVERSE

9.1 Enigmatically Embroidered = The Earth

9.2 Lucrative Life-giver = The Water

9.3 Blazing Brightness = The Fire

9.4 Flowing Force = The Air

9.5 Enchanting Ecstasy = The Ether

9.1

Enigmatically Embroidered = The Earth

Procreate things of enumerating weights, and gauging heights.
Nurturing both nutritious and nauseous; dynamic and static.
The radiant glamour pervasively clothed, even at the wretched sights,
Emerged from the womb of the Mighty at instants of a chaotically hectic.

Even in unfavored circumstances, unheard any cynicism about a mother.
Offspringing with absolute admiration, not expecting anything in return.
Never mindful of the injustice and disfiguring glitz triggering to bother,
Proficient in gratifying even the assailants, despite without any concern.

Wonderstruck by the impact experienced by the bizarre nature exhibited,
Realizing the disaster caused on the utilization of value and grandeur.
Yet worshiping the sacrifice rendered to the people, though inhibited,
Dare not to inquire the strength and the willpower intrinsic to endure.

Collaborating along with the other four fabulous and vital elements,
Mesmerize life with memory and hint to rectify certain moments!

9.2

Lucrative Life-giver = The Water

Water! Source of life and purification, leading to unexplained ecstasy,
Quench the physical thirst of all the living and longing creatures.
Soothe the sensuality, irrespective of any unpleasantly horrible fantasy,
Rude not power and pride but nurturing all equally hopeful futures.

In the sight of the Almighty, pervadingly omnipotent and omniscient,
Occupy a prominence due to the sustainable resourcefulness.
Realizing not, the innate nature of the intrinsically valued potent,
Silently in stillness, succor to experience the beautiful life in freshness.

Availed for varied needs, by the good as well as by so-called the bad,
Dilute not by the unpredictable nature, persistent altruism, and penchant.
Outsource the able capacity of resourcefulness by any inquisitive lad,
Create not only livelihood but selflessly spawning efficient merchant.

Qualities and quantities ascribed but match not the prominence possessed.
Not only cleanse the rusted mortals but illuminate the minute accessed!

9.3

Blazing Brightness = The Fire

Form Fire, due to the combination of oxygen, fuel, heat, and intensity,
The essential ingredient for survival; though, dangerous for extinction.
React with chemicals bursting off light, heat, and smoke, in high rapidity.
Pervade with smoke, harming the smooth respiratory inhalation.

The sun, volcanoes, and mines share as forms of arson, energy, and heat.
Ignited by this process, all machines function analogous to the process.
Known to the fact that bodies use "combustion" through metabolic synergy.
Sustain the bodies from the available oxygen and food consumed at recess.

Assist in molding and wielding ferociously to please the viewers' sight.
Char into ashes beyond identification with manmade gruesome accidents.
Aid in the formulation, whether delicious or tasteless, eases the daily plight.
Warn the influx ahead, defying the darers the consequences antecedents.

Indispensable for life, thrive in towards comfort zone with futurity.
Cause not any hazards affected by humans or wildlife with integrity.

© Irene Oleksiuk

9.4

Flowing Force = The Air

Element, made up of a variety of gases like nitrogen, and life-oxygen.
The carbon dioxide, krypton, and helium quantify the combination.
Invisible, felt the presence of comfort in the vicinity, full of nitrogen.
Occupies space due to the volume and pressure, even lifting up a nation.

Source of life to all, irrespective of caste, color, and creed among humans.
Whether bacterium or a gigantic mammal under the ocean or on the terrain.
Persists indispensably, yearned for succor for every moment, though yeoman.
Thank God for creating space for the air in the body to balance nature's reign.

Like a fish out of water, felt the absence in magnitude and arrogant capability.
Impossible to hold for a long time, even by admired kings, queens, and sages.
The mesmerizing melodies to the ears stimulate thought due to the air quality.
Sound – the essential necessities of life, hops by air from points to the edges.

Indeed great! Performs awesomely by interconnecting humans and plants.
Exchange of oxygen with carbon dioxide for existence like the ashplants.

9.5

Enchanting Ecstasy = The Ether

The element – the abode of cherubim and seraphs, proved elusive.
Unaffected by other elements, but not Ether due to untaintedness.
A liaison between the Anthropos to the preferred Deities of decisive.
Implicitly immortal, indestructible, and beyond the senses' awareness.

Abode of clouds, satiate the thirst of the desiccating green vegetation.
The savage of the terrain with torrential floods and tropical storms.
Fling the meteors and hurl whirlwinds, causing terrible destruction.
Showcase the rainbow in the sky, beautifully radiates the forms.

Humans share certain aspects of every element in the body's structure.
Represent the exit locations – ears, nostrils, and mouth of the existence.
Thrust missiles from the earth to the spaces beyond the gaze, capture.
The body animate the roles as per the responsibilities vested in essence.

Enthralling fields for men and gods to display magnificent power,
Way for the departed souls to the heavenly abode without any tower.

CHAPTER 10

VALUED VIRTUES AND VITIATING VICES

10.1 Choicest Charity = Vow of Chastity
10.2 Passionate Pledge = Vow of Poverty
10.3 Observed Obeisance = Vow of Obedience
10.4 Gracious Grants = 7 Gifts of the Holy Ghost
10.5 Dreaded Desires = 7 Deadly Sins

Choicest Charity = Vow of Chastity

10.1

Choicest Charity = Vow of Chastity

Desire – the resource of life: superior of the righteous qualities,
Harsh, though exhilarates to the voluptuous seventh heaven.
Impacts for the dearth of practice, signaling to atypical equalities.
Lauded by humankind for commitment, till snooped by the vile raven.

Imposed on the spouses, irrespective of doctrine, and diverse breeds.
Inflicted on the youth, till legitimately comprehend the consequences.
Consciously observed by the committed clerics of distinctive creeds,
Adhering to the unscripted sanctity, even realizing all its inherent nuances.

Appraised by individuals, valued by the siblings, and edified by the parents,
The virtue of chastity as a triumphant affirmation of filial attachment.
Asserted by critics, the most sensual perversions of the taunting torments,
By the ordinary as the order of natural life against inordinate enchantment.

Chastity! The honey in the rock for the heart; for the body, bitter Bittrex.
The favored souls, though the persistent struggle to imitate the Rex.

Passionate Pledge = Vow of Poverty

10.2

Passionate Pledge = Vow of Poverty

Economic paucity, affected by the power, placed everything in seconds,
Though struggling with the holy promise in day-to-day life maintenance.
Intimately observing the nuances like the shadow, despite persistent errands,
Invariably question the commitment professed earlier to its sustenance!

Does a mother, like an offspring, struggle with scarcity or among siblings?
Willfully embracing, "Poverty!" Part of the sacredly oriented magnanimity,
Regardless of unconditional limitedness, aside from ambiguous foundlings,
Swore to carry – the deliberate commitment genuinely with faithful nobility.

Not disturbed, but trusting the Mighty in all the earnestly struggling effort.
Exhilarated, invigorated, energized by His support in mystically apt pleasure.
As for the life, enthralled and entranced by worldly joyfulness support,
Rasping the waywardly provoked by its unintelligible and magic pressure!

Poverty, though frightened, the intrinsic value beyond comparison,
Aligning with the precepts, found the best beyond snapping separation.

Vow of Obedience

10.3

Observed Obeisance = Vow of Obedience

Obedience as the "mother of all virtues" for generating disposition.
Submission to the vow to God bases the moral order of virtue as slues.
The virtue determines between subordinate and superior interaction.
The human mind engrains and protects the other virtues and values.

As per the conscientiousness model, achievement, obligations
Revered by society and appreciated as a prominent prosocial behavior.
Noticed without surprise, by the Eastern collectivistic civilizations,
Even influencing ideologies and philosophies obedience as a warrior.

The obedience as a virtue infers a liberating truth of a man's pursuit.
Acquitting from attachment for the sake of God and man's salvation.
A committed life with a moral quest for a value beyond any lawsuit.
Imitating an inspired personality by heart via a holy revelation.

Obedience springs virtues – hope, faith, love, etc. along with justice.
Resides under justice accredited by the Almighty for daily practice.

The Seven Gifts of the Holy Spirit
Wisdom
Knowledge
Counsel
Fortitude
Understanding
Piety
Fear of the lord
Learn Religions

10.4

Gracious Grants = 7 Gifts of the Holy Ghost

Held the seven gifts of the Holy Spirit under the Catholic Tradition.
Theologians elaborate to strengthen the faith in God for benevolence.
The sanctifying gifts of the Spirit, secretly encrypted in the adoption.
In daily chores benefits glow in holiness and reaching transcendence.

Wisdom pertains to the knowledge of deific revelation for a truth.
Understating concerns the insight into the very heart for salvation.
Counsel, where God directs, a human conscience to ineffable faith.
Denoted fortitude as firmness of mind in dodging malicious motion.

Knowledge portrays an ability to judge matters of faith with fairness.
Piety, admiring God with filial affection, and saints with reverence.
Fear of God creates filial relationships with the divine with holiness.
The gifts of the Spirit enable to transcend the limitations of ignorance.

The traits of Jesus Christ, of the Trinity exhibited as an emolument.
To infuse the attributes into every believer through the sacrament.

7 DEADLY SINS
ENVY
ANGER
LUST
GLUTTONY
PRIDE
SLOTH
AVARICE

10.5

Dreaded Desires = 7 Deadly Sins

Termed SIN vitiating against the law, causing a person to feel guilty.
Infringing codes accepted by the majority populace in an observation.
"To err human, to forgive divine", signifies human flaw and frailty.
As humanoids exist sin too coexist like the haustorium adaptation.

Pride – an attitude of superiority, a pompous opinion of attainments.
Expressing a cynical connotation of great triumph and self-satisfaction.
Greed – a compulsive urge for bounty of wealth, power, and alignments.
Lust, a tangled desire against the chastity, and sexual gratification.

Envy – causing a sense of low self-esteem resulting from comparison.
Gluttony – an excessive food and drinks despite the feeling of contentment.
A choleric habit of body – Wrath, leading to covetousness and treason.
Sloth posits against diligence and invites God's resentment.

Sin exists in diverse ways like ignorance, murder, adultery, and theft.
But the "seven deadly sins" leads humans to corruption and bereft.

Glossary

Baptism: It is one of the seven sacraments administered in the Catholic Church.

Baisakhi: It is observed mainly by the Sikhs as a harvest festival as well as the birth of the Khalsa order by Guru Gobind Singh the tenth guru of Sikhism.

BBI: Bhubaneswar Biju Patnaik International Airport

BCE: Before Common Era

Bihu: It is the spring festival of Assam, and it is celebrated in three forms.

Bom Jesu Basilica: The only basilica in Goa, Basilica of Bom Jesus is a UNESCO World Heritage Site. The main attraction of this most popular church in Goa is that it houses the relics of St Francis Xavier.

Christmas: Christmas Day is celebrated on the 25th of December. It is a really important day, mainly for Christians, along with Easter. Christmas means – the word became man and dwelt among us. It means sharing divine love with humans. Christmas is celebrated not only among Christians but also by other faithful.

Circumcision: A sign of a covenantal relationship with God the Almighty among the Jews and Muslims.

City of Joy: Kolkata has been described as 'City of Joy' by French author Dominique Lapierre. Kolkatans know how to enjoy – be it Durga Puja, Christmas, or New Year celebrations.

Diwali: It is the Hindu festival of lights with its variations also celebrated in other Indian religions. It symbolizes the spiritual "victory of light over darkness, good over evil, and knowledge over ignorance".

Durga Puja: It is an annual Hindu festival dedicated to the Goddess Durga. It is celebrated all over the world by the Hindu community, but it is particularly popular and traditionally celebrated in the Indian states.

Eucharist: The origin of the term "Eucharist" is from the Greek word – eucharistia, which means thanksgiving. It is the faith of the Christians that during the celebration of the Eucharist, bread and wine become the Body and Blood of Jesus Christ through the power of the Holy Spirit and the instrumentality of the priest. The changing process is known as 'transubstantiation'.

Gudi Padwa: It is the Marathi New Year. It gets its name from two words – 'Gudi', which means a flag or emblem of Hindu Lord Brahma, and 'Padwa' means the first day of the phase of the moon, and the festival marks the beginning of the harvest season and is celebrated with much fervor and enthusiasm in the state of Maharashtra.

Holi: It is a spring festival celebrated throughout India as the Festival of Colors. It involves the throwing of 'Gulal' (colored powder) and water. It is celebrated everywhere indicating all about love, goodness, and welcoming positive energy back into your life.

Holy Spirit: As per the Christian faith, the Holy Spirit, or Holy Ghost, is believed to be the third person of the Trinity, a triune God manifested as God the Father, God the Son, and God the Holy Spirit, each being God.

HYD: Hyderabad

Initiation: A religious practice that is conventionally and conveniently followed in different religions.

ID: Identification or identity

Kasu, Duttu, Tonka, and Rupiah: The English work – Money is equal to Kasu in Tamil, Duttu in Kannada, Tonka in Odia, and Rupiah in Hindi.

Kharif and Rabi Crops: are mostly used to indicate the right time to sow and raise a particular crop. Kharif crops are sown at the beginning of the rainy season and are also known as monsoon crops. These crops are harvested in September and October. Some examples of Kharif crops are rice, bajra, groundnut, cotton, etc. The sowing season generally starts around November and the crops are harvested between March and April which is springtime in the region. They are also known as winter crops. Some of the common examples of major Rabi crops grown in India are wheat, mustard, barley, green peas, sunflower, coriander, cumin, etc.

Krishna Janmashtami: It is an annual Hindu festival that celebrates the birth of Krishna, the eighth avatar of Vishnu.

Lohri: It is Punjabi folk festival, celebrated primarily in Northern India. Lohri marks the end of winter and is a traditional welcome of longer days and the sun's journey to the Northern Hemisphere by people in the northern region of the Indian subcontinent.

Lord Jesus Christ's Apparitions: The Gospels state that on the first day of the week after the death, Jesus appeared to his disciples, followers, and believers in various ways at different places.

MAA: Madras International Meenambakkam Airport

Mandovi & Zuari: The Mandovi and the Zuari are the two principal rivers in the state of Goa. Mandovi is known as the largest and most important river in Goa. Zuari is the longest river in the state of Goa.

MC (Missionaries of Charity): The Missionaries of Charity is a Catholic religious institute of consecrated life of Pontifical Right for Women aimed at wholehearted free service to the poorest of the poor. It was established in 1950 by Mother Teresa, now known in the Catholic Church as Saint Teresa of Calcutta.

Navratri: It is an annual Hindu festival observed in honor of the goddess Durga, an aspect of Adi Parashakti, the supreme goddess.

Panchami: It is a festival of Hindus and Sikhs that marks the beginning of preparations for the spring season. It is celebrated by people in various ways depending on the region.

Pongal: Pongal (பொங்கல்), also referred to as Thai Pongal (தைப்பொங்கல்), is a multi-day Hindu harvest festival celebrated by Tamils in India and Sri Lanka. The three days of the Pongal festival are called Bhogi Pongal, Surya Pongal, and Mattu Pongal. Some Tamils celebrate a fourth day of Pongal known as Kanum Pongal.

Raksha Bandhan: It means as "bond of protection." It is celebrated the love between a brother and sister. On this day, a sister ties a threaded amulet, known as a 'rakhi', around a brother's wrist, honoring their relationship. The bracelet symbolizes the brother's oath to protect his sister throughout her life, and the sister's prayers and blessings for the protection and wellbeing of her brother. He then gives her a gift, signifying his acceptance of this duty.

Rama Navami: It is a Hindu festival that celebrates the birth of Rama, one the most popularly revered deities in Hinduism, also known as the seventh avatar of Vishnu.

Sankranti: It refers to the transmigration of the sun from one zodiac to another in Indian astronomy. Each Sankranti is marked as the beginning of a month in the sidereal solar calendars followed in the states of India.

Shard Purnima: It is a religious festival celebrated on the full moon day of the Hindu lunar month of Ashvin (September to October), marking the end of the monsoon season.

Tamil New Year: Tamil New Year also called Puthandu (புத்தாண்டு) or Tamil varusha pirappu (தமிழ் வருட பிறப்பு) is the celebration of the Tamil New Year as per the Tamil calendar.

Ugadi: Ugadi is the Telugu New Year Day which begins in the month of The Chaitra (April or May) which heralds joy, peace, and prosperity.

Vedas: Generally understood the religious texts of Hinduism. It literally means "knowledge," that found in the oldest texts of Hinduism. It is stated that they are derived from the ancient Indo-Aryan culture of the Indian Subcontinent and began as an oral tradition that was passed down through generations before finally being written in Vedic Sanskrit between 1500 and 500 BCE.

Vasant

Vishu: It is a cultural festival celebrating the Malayali New Year in Kerala, Tulu Nadu, and Mahi of India.

Vows: A vow is a promise or oath. A vow is used as a promise, a promise solemn rather than casual. It is performed during marriages. Vows are taken by religious persons to live a committed life namely vows of poverty, chastity, and obedience.

Yama Raj: According to Hinduism, he is believed as the God of death and justice, responsible for the dispensation of law and punishment of sinners in his abode, Naraka.

PLEASE NOTE: The glossary points are referred from the website.

Profile of the Author

Dr. Fr. Arokiya Dass V, S.J. is a Jesuit, teaching in the school of Commerce, XIM University, Bhubaneswar, Odisha, India. Presently, He is the Chief Finance Officer (CFO) and Deputy Registrar in XIM University. He is a hard worker; rule-abiding in nature; very sociable and jovial. He loves the teaching profession passionately as himself. He has a soft corner towards the poor and the marginalized. He is very secular in his approach. He has friends from different walks of life. He has rich and diverse experience in the academic arena. He is down to earth by nature hence colleagues and coworkers approach him without any hesitation. He converses in a half dozen Indian languages. Though he has a PhD in Finance, yet has done Bachelor of Philosophy (B.Ph.) and Bachelor of Theology (B.Th.). He holds a diploma in Indian Classical Dance. He delivers discourses on spiritual topics, seminars and orientations to the teachers and corporates.

www.ingramcontent.com/pod-product-compliance
Lightning Source LLC
Chambersburg PA
CBHW030023260726
48782CB00025B/297

9798894153124